BLOOD | SALT | SPRING

BLOOD | SALT | SPRING

Hannah Lavery

Polygon

First published in Great Britain in 2022 by
Polygon, an imprint of Birlinn Ltd.

Birlinn Ltd
West Newington House
10 Newington Road
Edinburgh EH9 1QS

9 8 7 6 5 4 3 2 1

www.polygonbooks.co.uk

Copyright © Hannah Lavery, 2022

The right of Hannah Lavery to be identified as the author
of this work has been asserted in accordance with the
Copyright, Designs and Patents Act 1988.

All rights reserved. No part of this publication may be reproduced,
stored, or transmitted in any form, or by any means electronic,
mechanical or photocopying, recording or otherwise, without
the express written permission of the publisher.

ISBN 978 1 84697 607 0
EBOOK ISBN 978 1 78885 490 0

British Library Cataloguing-in-Publication Data
A catalogue record for this book is available
from the British Library.

The publisher gratefully acknowledges investment from
Creative Scotland towards the publication of this book.

Typeset in Verdigris MVB by Polygon, Edinburgh
Printed and bound in Great Britain by Clays Ltd, Elcograf S.p.A.

For Beldina Odenyo

CONTENTS

BLOOD
I have rubies sewn in . . .

Questions of Percentage	2
The Galley Kitchen	3
The Long Walk	4
Cartographer's Trap	7
Pocket Money	8
Inheritance	9
Make a Den	10
Last in the Film	11
Backwards	12
The System, 1985	14
My Mum Wears Pink Lipstick	16
Leeds Cathedral	18
Six of One and Half a Dozen of the Other	19
Filled Notebooks	20
Halfling	22
Grieving	24
Remix for the Brown Girl	25
15th December 2014	26

SALT
Now only the supervised showing of skin

Fake News	28
Untitled	30
Black Cat	31
Spilt Milk	34
We'll Be Polar Bears	35
Fragments, 2021	37
The Way of Things	44
Everyday Racism	45
The Anti-Racist Working Group	46
Hush Now (Shitty Brown)	47
Scotland, You're No Mine	49
Thirty Laughing Emojis	51
I Sang You Rainbow Songs	53
Abigail Says She's a Witch	54
The Wild Names Us	56
Plastic Binoculars	57
Japanese Mountain	58
Kissing Toads	61
You Missed the Birds	62
Dear Mum	63
Daily Exercise (and Shopping Online)	65
Proposal	66
Snowdrops	67
Lapwings	68

SPRING
I would be powered by only you

Firefly	70
Flying Bats	71
Bears	73
Outwith (Writing Workshop on Zoom)	75
Rewrites	77
Poetry Platforms	78
Chapel	80
The Perfect Shade	81
Glorious	82
Mind the Gap	83
Missed Trains	84
Leaves Fall Gold	85
Murmuration Passes	87
Broken Shell	88
Day of Our Dead	89
Cassandra	90
Mum's Things	91
Them Apples	92
Preserving the Sun	93
Fifteen Year Honey	94
The Poet and Her Son	95
It's This	97
Green	98
Acknowledgements	99
A note on the author	101

BLOOD

I have rubies sewn in . . .

QUESTIONS OF PERCENTAGE

are you done
with the percentages – yet?

which side are we
falling down on – then?

THE GALLEY KITCHEN

In her narrow kitchen
above the pinboard
with the calendar
from the Chinese takeaway
and a family photo that came in the post
she imagines a picture of the Pope
(beside a picture of the Queen).

Watching over her
as she brings the soup
up to boil. Gazing upon her
as she adds in cannonballs
of peppercorn.

THE LONG WALK

I have rubies sewn in, but he
says, that this is where I am
this room with its three-bar heat.

In our afternoon stupor, Bing Crosby
emerges in low hum, and we
sit here in this cardboard house
tea drinking and bickering like cats

but I have these blisters buried deep
and a whip of the fronds on my back
and even in this central heat *I am cold*

sweat. In my hand, I am still
holding Aunty's tiffin tin, still
putting off the chore of serving her
lunch in her cane chair

in her golden throne – *Buddha Aunt*.
I light candles in the cathedral
incense in the chapel, hold ledger

and spice. Swing the tiffin offering
before removing silk slip, pushing over my ayah
to run free – calling for my brother but

met by Mother Jamaica at the shore
reaching in to our great ruby days
with old shackles

she burns sage.
Takes my dying brother
from my arms

(leaving me his hand always to hold).

This handing down of corpses.
We wear bones. Smuggle
them with the golden bangles. Each
one an inheritance to hold

as our neighbours lay down in the ditch
to die. Our black crone pulls at the tree
handing my mother an urging of fronds

for when they put us out like rats
in their kitchen, like bats in their attic

(she hands down the palm switch).

In this refuge, he croons, this is the end
of my story, but I carry these blisters
and hold out this lash of bound leaf . . .

He gets another pot of tea and fetches
the packet of McVities. I will like this one
he announces, and we spend the rest of our day

watching my war made real
with white faces. I say it wasn't
like that, except the planes.

The planes were really bombed
before we could get to them. We
really did have to walk. *Did you*

know? I tell my granddaughter
my mother made a switch from a palm tree
to whip me up the road when I wanted
to lie down and die

You *wanted to die?*

She cries.

CARTOGRAPHER'S TRAP

She always loved a fresh start
like she always loved fresh sheets
a new dress and the start of the school year

but she never thought they would leave
and when it came, *the leaving*
it was not fresh but stale.

She pulled all she was behind her
and left. They all did. Leaving
only weight. A dent of their dragging.

Yes, she always loved a fresh start
but this leaving was bloodshot
snot faced, tear streaked. A leaving

without orchestra.

Her land hidden in her knickers
a secret wee piss stain.

POCKET MONEY

He never had a wallet
kept his money like dirty hankies
stuffed in back pockets

was always losing fivers
money slipping away like eels
to be found stranded

in sofa cracks
dragging knuckles
stuck to the arses of jockeys.

Stuffed in back pockets
falling out, like family.

INHERITANCE
For my sisters

The Kingfisher visits us
as the snow comes down
like Christmas day
watching us, as we flap like gulls
at the crusts of all this perfect white.

The snow melts – *as it was bound to*
leaving more bog to cross
and we try (as we always do)
in our mothers' shoes.

Ahead the Kingfisher creates
a kaleidoscope for us
a guide of sorts (or warning?)
Reminding us of halcyon days

of how we loved him once
so much, we called him Zeus
so much, we woke the Gods.

MAKE A DEN

As a child, I would hide under tables with you.
She would throw blankets over to make a den.
We would create an entrance through a chair

Bring a torch.

I would dare you to bring snacks from the kitchen.
I would remember those half-sister days
when back home without you, that longing for you

A dark blanket.

As a child, I would hide under the table with you
in the part of your sitting room that was *the dining room.*
He would throw blankets.

A ground sheet

he found in the shed, leave us there hidden
while he shouted at the horses on the telly.
We would spend all morning bringing in
the essentials.

Make a barricade

to keep the others out. Maybe, we made a sign.
I remember torchlight. Even then I was missing you.
As a child, I would

Hide under the table.

LAST IN THE FILM

We sit, two dirty angels in our Sunday best
hoisted up to sit pretty as a picture. Holiday snap

on seaweed rock. He demands smiles
as tears crawl – insects up our legs.

We smile – hold. Hands on our laps.
Together, we let the sun wash out

the rocks behind us
our angel-face glare

an instant caught in the instamatic.

Replacing our smiles
quick as a flash
with that sudden truth

stuck down with the others
precious number 24 of the roll
and he will know, even when we fight

to remember, the tsunami he brought
just moments before

the gulls – the shore – the hushed cry.

BACKWARDS

She corrals us brown kids
into *Remedial*, muted
in our mothers' tongues
though here, it's only
my father they see.

Months pass as *Miss*
attempts to convince
me, that a d is made up
of a bouncing ball and a bat

'Two bs make one d?
A bouncing ball?
Is that not three?'

(Oh I see now, this is where I lose my faith)

My mother fights for me
screams, I don't belong *(her mother tongue)*
'She reads *Anne of Green Gables*!'
I do. Not that it matters *(or maybe
it does)* when in the playground
wi knees scuffed from falling—

'It matters not a jot', channelling Anne
for I am on a pony and trap with Matthew
travelling the white way of delight
passing by the lake of shining waters.

And those are not school railings but
the wild wood and those are not
spitting lads *with sweaty cocks* but
wild boar or *Nazi soldiers running down the line*

and I am not a girl
I am sea mist
the morning harr
Poison gas
floating between
dancing upon
bouncing my ball

swinging my *fucking* bat.

THE SYSTEM, 1985

She remembers
the sum of their thinking

White mother + brown child
= lack of maternal attachment.

I remember
packed bag

I remember
panic

I remember
shock

I remember
restraint

Bodies pile on
on my little brown back

with its

'Caribbean Curve'
pressed out flat

Mum!

I remember
running to high wall

Sprinting free
of hospital corner

Mum!

I remember
dead weight.

Mum!

I remember
I was seven.

MY MUM WEARS PINK LIPSTICK

I'd say you laid me in a sugar-pink shawl but I can't be sure.
You with your sugar-pink lipstick smile – like that sugar-pink dress
that the Aunt Betty doll with her porcelain pink cheeks wore.

Did we put her upon a cane chair or was it Great-Granny's chair?
That you wrapped in sugar-pink and powder-blue fabric wi cushions
and curtains matching. The sugar-pink of the Knickerbocker Glory

we had after the dentist, matching the pink of it to our scoured gums
and the underside of his palms. We brought out sugar-pink icing
for the Saturday tea, an indoor picnic, watching the A-Team.

Stuffing our faces wi sugar-pink Turkish delight, your sugar-pink
lips marking, claiming me. Mornings, I sat at the end of your bed
watching cartoons and reaching under your duvet to tickle

your pink pink toes. Now, I think it is not pink but peach
and looking back, not so sweet but fresh. It was a peach
and it was peachy skin and peach melba and it was peaches

we ate from the pedalo sellers that time in Greece, peaches
the size of tennis balls, collected from the waves, your peach
skin wet with the juice, beautiful peach skin turning shade deeper

that sugar-pink lipstick dripping on my cheek. I was melon.
A melon colour. Yellow like my yellow towelling shorts with the go
faster stripes. My yellow skin, sandy like your yellow hair before

Henna-red, Body Shop paste, turning my hands as green
as our kitchen walls, where we danced on Sundays to the Top 40.
Sugar-pink you and me, your melon, melanated girl

and sometimes the sugar-pink fell like paint, like raindrops.
Like rainbow sugar drops found in pockets. My mum
wears sugar-pink lipstick and I find the stains of it

the sweet sticky marks of it – everywhere.

LEEDS CATHEDRAL

My mum and I come down
on the train from Dunbar.

We get a Priest to bless you.
In the morgue, I weep over your body

with a broken voice, Mum calls
you a *stupid bloody man*.

I light candles for you
in Leeds Cathedral

(repeat ad infinitum)

SIX OF ONE AND HALF A DOZEN OF THE OTHER

Eyes down. Top deck. Mis-
step. *Paki!* Misfit in two step.

Count me in, count me out
match me up, hand me down
Happy Family?

In the half-caste union
match your shade.

Leave if you're the lightest.
Leave if you're the darkest.

Leave.

Come in with that skin, we have hooks
to hang it. We will make a whore of you yet.

Put you there for the first timers, for their practice runs.

Gaslight. Harsh light. Searchlight. No light.
Too light. No right. Take your folding chair

and stack it by the door.

Nan tells you about a sun, so warm
she can still see it on your skin.

FILLED NOTEBOOKS

1.
My mother would love you, he said and Julie preened. Her hair whipping up to a halo. What about her? Julie said. He looked at her – all tie dyed top and beige skin. Her? Her, I would fuck.

2.
There was no denying he was beautiful. That he wanted her. That alone they talked of their fathers.

3.
He called her his Black Magic Woman and sang the song to her as he ripped off her training bra, biting her brown tit so hard, she hit out and pulled at his blond curls.

4.
He missed his father – violently. She missed her father – worried she had forgotten his face. They spent two hours walking ten minutes, sat together on the beach, sharing secrets. When she finally got home, she had lost her keys.

5.
They spent afternoons learning each other like a test. It became too much, he said, and he went back to playing basketball and skateboarding on the Prom.

6.
She put on black eyeliner and listened to new music. He came back for her – carrying chains.

7.
She fought back, but he laid her out like meat at the market – offered them a cut.

8.
Shared with his boys, the secrets of her, along with joints, porn mags and ninety-minute mixtapes.

9.
Feeling free, in laughing packs, they called her a slut and threw eggs at her bedroom window. Drunk and horny on Saturday nights, they asked him for more of her before running home to their mothers erect and panting – covered in her shattered shell.

10.
When he was without them, he would whisper softly through the night to her.

11.
Seeing her brown limbs through her fence, they brought cider to her as an offering. Invaded her day and took the sun. Drunk, she danced for them like their marionette. They passed the strings between them until he took hold. Oh, how he made her dance – as they peered desperate through the keyhole.

12.
Laughing, they staggered home for their tea. Laughing, as she crawled away from herself. So loud were their cheers when he caught up to them – zipping up his fly.

13.
She filled notebooks. Bled the day into a bedpan.

14.
He practised his rebellion on her skin.
Hunched over his twelve string
mimicking the blues.

HALFLING

I've never been tall
although I think

I may have been
when I was wee.

I used to dance
in the streets.

Sing on buses
ride high

on Daddy's shoulders

but growing up
it gets you

smaller in ways.

Dads leave, and maybe
och, I don't know

you find you take
up less room.

Sometimes, I say
I'd be a halfling

It's true, I think
I'd rather stay small

*walking unnoticed
by monsters.*

GRIEVING

Today I am
driftwood. Scum.

Stuff found in pockets.
Dirt under fingernails.

I am hiding
under rock.

REMIX FOR THE BROWN GIRL

They go on remixing
my mixed blood
my fractured sense

to be newly named
parsed and recorded. Gag
my many moving mouths

until I'm hanging upside down.

Sweet trumpeter, John Blanke
plays, *it's such a waste
of all that we had*

(Of all that I ever had).

15TH DECEMBER 2014
(My father's funeral)

Meeting you again, in all the photos they brought
like ashes to your wake, and whilst they cooed over
the boy you were, after khow and chicken curry
with a cigarette taken from my almost-sister
another from your almost-third-wife, a rum to go
and with a last look back, I took what I had had
and threw it to the wind. It did not go
but settled instead, to be cinders on my back
it followed me home (you all followed me home).

SALT

Now only the supervised showing of skin

FAKE NEWS

I want to lie in wait for you
kick you in the shins.

Trap you in a basement
feed you your eyeballs
through the gap in the door.

I want you to howl
until you're hoarse.

Resurrect your demons.
Kill your angels.
Hack your profile.

I want to drink cheap Prosecco
from the skulls of your children.

Piss on your perspective
let it mix. Brew
a craft beer. Distil
a boutique gin.

I want to laugh at you
in your underwear.

Lose you in a maze.
Chase you with a shotgun.

Bring on the zombie apocalypse.

Ride the four horsemen
through your living room

feed them your pets.

I want to bring you cups
of tar with seagull wings

tell you it's your morning coffee.
Feed you your neighbours' food waste.

Take you out and shoot you
burn your libraries

shred your history
pull you from your grave

make you dance for me.

UNTITLED

Smile, like you were taught
it will be done, in minutes
then you can go home.

BLACK CAT
4 *November 2015*

Did you know it would rain today?

Light flashes, KRAVE, light flashes, KRAVE
and you all gather in a smokers' huddle.

Worship here
you are wonderfully made.

Here, they don't seem to walk alone
in gaggles, pairings, in matching black .

Bald head to the rain, with his heavy bag
walks different now, from that lost peacock walk of his youth

and as another preening teen walks by, he stops in the middle of the road
to let him pass. Sighs and then walks on, his bag lopsiding him.

Worship here
you are wonderfully made.

It is her job to open the church but she has to go back
for change for the parking meter. Her church has now diversified

to eclectic accommodation round the back, gym, office space, flat to rent.

And in another city they hide . . .

But here, it's the rain that bows heads and clears the streets.

Here, my East Coast ear must re-tune to *a storm is coming*
with the *coming*, going high up over my head.

And here, a red car follows a taxi with a sign
illuminating tropical beach with the words

Get out of here

follows bus to
Knightswood

follows bus to
Paisley

bus to
Drumchapel

bus to
Eastwood.

Worship here
you are wonderfully made.

A woman smokes a joint whilst she waits.

And in another city they hide
behind their wooden shutters

their cat prowling abandoned
outside on the ledge.

Cutting in surreal
on rolling news footage

moving with grace, above
the banner tape screaming

Terror in Paris

looping, repeating, looping back . . .

Staring out on a Glasgow street, thinking
about a wee black cat on a Paris balcony.

SPILT MILK

That night we'd gone to bed.
We'd had enough of waiting up for history
and we knew how this would play out...
They'd been up already, stuffed their bowls with chocolate hoops
and I was too tired to tell them to watch the milk
 so I was on my knees when
I registered something was off
  a shift in the drone.
I let the milk spread at whim.
     Fuck!
          I think I cried.
Thought of Jo Cox
               bleeding out on that Northern Street.
Wading through the milk
    David Cameron was resigning.
I was looking out their shoes.
        I shouted up to my him
  It's all fucked! They've gone and fucking fucked it.
My three splashed in the rush of milk
now filling up our hall. I left them to it
to put the news on the telly.
           His big moon face was on the run. The circus had come.
I took the heads off all their Lego figures
lined them up and blew over each one.
   Jesus Christ!
          He said taking my hand.
Our children must have opened the door
the spilt milk was escaping

(Our neighbours were being washed away).

WE'LL BE POLAR BEARS
25 January 2020

Burns Night already
but I've just spotted three
Christmas trees in their windows.

Och, mibbe just students
still to return, to find
Christmas like old wine bottles.

Ghosts mocking them
for their seasonal decadence
that brotherhood of man.

Or stubborn defiance?
I mean, are we no, now wishing
we could wind back the clock?

Can we not just remain?

A Christmas tree?
Just three still in the stair
saying on you go, I'm nae fae going . . .

We'll be Polar bears
on that last piece of ice.
Bedraggled, bedecked wi fairy lights

drooping all Raggedy Ann. Tinseled
in a state of hope. My train is moving again
and the next block is in January darkness

but those three trees
a slut's disgrace, a drunken fuck you, last orders
aye? But this pint snuck out under your fake fur

defiance!

Burns Night already, we are well into 2020
but I just spotted three Christmas trees
out my train window. Ack! I don't know

it just felt like something.

FRAGMENTS, 2021

1.
We took what we were given
and spun a web

for them to catch us in
wore it like a crown

dressed in it
like it was gold, like it was silk

and not a trap.

2.
And we didn't go out and protest
because our children were restless
and our mothers were failing

and our work was calling
and our bills needed paying
but we took to the night

for just a moment
to breathe

before turning back
and walking home

she was just walking home.

3.
I'm done.
I'm not switching on.
I'm not turning up.
I'm not tuning in
I'm not holding on
to your bloody hand
– not today.

I'm not going to rise up.
I'm not going to stand up
and fist up and kneel down
I'm not taking this on.
I'm not fighting
your opinions.
Not today.

I'm not coming in.
I'm drop weight.
I'm pit bound.
I'm levelling down
each level down

He took us
whilst we slept, whilst we walked, whilst we . . .
I'm in the pit
buried neck deep
I'm wi the devil – today.

When you called, pal
I was here
nailed to the cross, mate.
building a pyre, mate
collecting all the fire, mate

winding rope to the trees
mother?

I'm not going out today
I'm not coming over.

I'm swinging wi all the . . .
Swinging wi all my dead girls.

I'm not getting up
I'm pulled in

drawn drapes down
drawn crepe gown
drawn clown face
drawn corpse bride

I'm drowning in pulled sheets

Holding off bedlam
marked beldam

I'm not going
not today.

I'm down in the mud swamp.
I'm sleeping in dark pit.

I'm sleeping
in bright flash (light).

I'm drowning
in pulled sheets.

4.
She stands
for another year, in a chamber of echoes
prepares to list the dead, they cut to an old man
in a hall of mirrors, before she even finishes

saying their names.

5.
In a dream
my grandmother
appeared

gold bangles
red silk
lily of the valley.

She handed me rosemary
I took it
I took her hand

my inheritance
handed down in larch box.

Find your coven
she whispered.

6.
If we were real

we would be as tall as statues.
As permanent as a street name

as strong as a building
named after our sister

built for our sisters to speak

monuments would rise
to meet the birds

(our ghost women).

THE WAY OF THINGS
March 2020

If this is the way of things now
I choose morning coffee with you.

Drunk in our garden
or on our sofa when it rains.

We will drink it slowly
silently.

If this is the way of things now
I choose silence with you.

We will mute everyone beyond us
and let in only birdsong.

We will turn it away
as it walks up our path

looking again for my father
you already claimed him

you wore out his heart
left us with silence.

Silence, I drink my coffee in
write my words from
raise my children in

(but still, you carry on killing him).

EVERYDAY RACISM

I insist you take a snack with you.
Remind you to wear a helmet.
Fill your water bottle.
Wait . . . Listen
for the screech of your brakes
as you cycle too fast at the corner.

An hour or so passes
I've not been listening.
I just watch her
in the top right box of the Zoom room
stare through a window out of shot . . .
The light catching her blonde hair and

it is her view I'm imagining, when my stomach falls
like a fairground ride, but a long moment
passes before I hear your bike drop
on our path I leave them their conversation continues
a drone under . . .

I hold you
as I've always held you
letting you find that familiar comfort
that regulation in my . . .

Hush – now. Hush – now. Hush – now. Hush – now—
Mum, they called me a . . .
Hush now. Hush now. Hush—

THE ANTI-RACIST WORKING GROUP

They apologise for their lateness (and the one that should really be here, won't be here). *Don't worry, it's fine.* This is the first meeting of the anti-racist working group.

adjective: **befuddled**
>   1. *unable to think clearly; confused or perplexed.*
>   '*even in my befuddled state I could see that they meant trouble*'

He worries that thinking of him like that is racist. *Black?* Her face and my face. We share a look which even on Zoom we both recognise.

verb
past tense: **befuddled**; past participle: **befuddled**
>   1. make (someone) unable to think clearly.
>   'the logic used to arrive at this conclusion befuddles me'

We arrange to talk after the meeting is done. We wonder why *they* thought *they* had anything useful to say. What were *they* thinking? she says. What the hell was the thinking?

Befuddled. Befuddle. Befuddling

We sort of laugh, wonder how long it will be, before *they* move on. Wonder, if *they* are starting to realise, that *they* don't want to give anything away.

Hush now. Hush now. Hush—

HUSH NOW (SHITTY BROWN)

The parents were very sorry
this is not our son. Not *their* son

(it's mine).

We will make sure
they never change alone.

Now only the supervised
showing of skin.

Her face flashes irritation
at parents' evening

what a fuss I'm making.

Looking past me
his parents

(she tells me)

say it's very unusual for him
to act this way.

Do you know his mother
cried when she heard?

We will supervise them now
when they change for gym.

This is not like our son, they say.

I cry
when he's asleep

after my white friend
... *you know it's just what kids* ...

This is not like our son
(it's mine)

It's my son, undressing
by the teacher in fear

they will become again
so unlike themselves.

SCOTLAND, YOU'RE NO MINE

(you were no his)
and I don't want you.

So go ahead, say I don't belong
wi your sepia-tinged cross eye sweeping
over all that swept-away, blood-stained, sweat-
        stained sugar for your tablet.

Ya macaroon. Ya rotten
gobby, greedy, thieving bastard you
sitting atop a that shite and broken bones
weeping
        Poor me.

Fuck you! I will dance jigs on your flags
blue 'n' white; blue, white 'n' red.
It doesne matter but, ya wee chancer!

Fuck! For making us complicit
handing us whip and chains, an officer's coat
a civil-service pen, a Queen to love.

And lay me out, I love you
with your mountain thyme and all your coorie in.
And you can say, I dinnae belong to you – go on

– but I am limpet stuck on you.
So fuck you for no seeing one of your own.
I will, here. I will spill, here

my blood and your secrets
bleed into you, root and earth
and you, forever, pagan, will, in the spill

and the seep, see all you really are.
So fuck you, my sweet forgetful Caledonia.
With love, fuck you.

THIRTY LAUGHING EMOJIS
'Woman' was the test, but not every woman seemed to qualify.
                                                    Angela Davis

We have sixty-three mutual friends.

Status Update: *Woke? Enough already!*
>Comment (mutual friend): *Do you know the origins of the word?*
>Reply: *Quite aware of origins. Don't need to be 'educated' thanks.*

We have sixty-two mutual friends.

Status Update: *Interesting to see the folk at BLM protests are the same ones who were on here complaining about Cummings. Happy to break lockdown when the political mood music changes.*
>Comment: *This is what I have been trying to articulate. Thanks for this.*
>Comment (WOC mutual friend): *Hey!*

No further comments. We have forty mutual friends.

(WOC friend screenshots, sends to her WOC friend on Messenger: *Seen this?: You okay?: Not really.*)

Status Update: *Yes, I am white but I'm also a woman. Privilege – really?*
>Comment: *I really worry about these ideas of privilege, so divisive.*
>Comment: *I've certainly never had any privilege and resent folk with postgrads telling me I have.*
>Comment: *I grew up on Pot Noodles!*
>Reply: *Chicken and mushroom?*

Twenty Laughing Emojis. One hundred comments on Pot Noodle flavours.

Status Update: *Use your personal anecdotes to silence any challenge. This my friends is the depressing level of intellectual debate in 2020. Now let me tell you about how the big girls were mean to me at school.*

Fifty Laughing Emojis. Ten personal anecdotes in support.

Status Update: *Let's face it, this Karen thing is just another way of silencing and humiliating women. There, I said it.*

Sixty Likes.

> Comment (Karen): *Can't begin to tell you how irritating this is.*
> Reply: *Maybe you should ask for their manager?*

Thirty Laughing Emojis

I SANG YOU RAINBOW SONGS

We learnt the colours on woodland walks. Like the sun or the big light, I was a tatty moth drawn to you – *shining sun*.

Suddenly, it seems you have turned from me (but still I am flapping wings in search of you).

Yesterday, I came home to find you wrapped in rainbow flags. You said he called you a faggot in the changing rooms.

At 10 p.m. last night, we were still watching telly, we ate all the chocolate. I am not sure this was the best way to deal with your pain.

You didn't want to go to school today.

Mothering you my love
is knowing before you do
but still not knowing.

Still not knowing.

ABIGAIL SAYS SHE'S A WITCH

They are resurrecting the witch
pulling charred corpses from the pit
for reburial (and easy metaphor).

The oddballs. The freaks wearing
the devil's mark, gather at the gate
hands held, carrying sage.

I am a witch
Abigail says (barring the way)
to them, to Tituba
rising out from our memory

(her finger pointing, her fist raised).

I am a witch
Abigail echoed in likes
in inch by column inch

I am true
and they gather with
proclamations.

General
the troops for the ritual
purge.

In all this cutting down
firewood, new pyres.

In all this throwing of rocks
flint, old fire.

In free speech thrown
the struck are

silenced
(as they always were)

in their
monster mask
hangman's hood
shackle
millstone.

But Abigail says she's the witch
I am the hunted

is handed pitchfork
tiki torch, the stage, her flowers.
Her applause, her encore.

Brava! Brava!

All hail the witch!
All hail! All hail the witch!

THE WILD NAMES US

Smell maker.
Noise erupter.
Den mother.

Alpha – *fuck!*

Tail less.
Wing less.
Fur Shaver.

Mouse.

Baby maker.
Corpse hoarder.
Nest builder.
Terminator.

Ramrod.

Blood matted.
Skin shedder.
Shape shifter.

Death cult.

Time watcher.
Life bender.
Street walker.
Shy shagger.

Sea creature.

PLASTIC BINOCULARS

1.
He seemed to find it amusing
how distressed I became when
the seagull killed the pigeon outside
the *Scottish Poetry Library*.

In the pages we were charged
to protect, I could find nothing
to save the bird on the cobbles.

I flew around the room
battering at the windows.

2.
We'd been feeding the birds
anxiously. Shouting at cats
all that Spring Lockdown. Quick
study we became, learnt the names
from the *Ladybird Book of Garden Birds*.

Used plastic binoculars to see what we could already see.

Easter Sunday, I spotted another thing – beautiful. So unusual
we needed the internet. We stood captives at the patio doors.
It's a Woodpecker! she said in her paper bonnet. We spent a week
looking out for it – then went back to shouting at cats.

3.
The new neighbours from the slightly newer homes
post a picture of two roe deer in their tarmac drive.
We are silent in our slightly older homes remembering
the fields, the felled wood.

JAPANESE MOUNTAIN

Your curtains are shit
they let the light in

light too harsh to sleep in.

I've been awake all night
curled a question mark
in your sheets. My words

and your words stacked
beside me on your pillow.
It is 4 a.m. on a Thursday.

I am sinking. All around me
I resist the thought. Talk
myself out of . . .

I call it love, but maybe
it's only seeing you.

Why do you do this?
I don't know.

This thing I call love
which you call another thing.

An unwelcome thing

the feelings I feel that I had not meant to feel
the feelings I feel that I had thought flowers

that I had thought beautiful
that I had thought rare.

And I leave you
taking my ugly.

I leave you relieved
to be relieved of me.

What am I to you now?

Broken record.
Discord to our
perfect pitch. Score
marked down. A blot
in the copy book.

Shame she comes
to me. My familiar

with gut punch
with her bruised

blooms for me
with weeds for me

and I put them in water
till water is yellow then wrap them
in newspaper till they crisp to bookmark

bookmarking words you gave me, along
with a picture of a Japanese mountain
its beauty I didn't understand.

Too undefined.
To be honest, it frightened me a little.

You slipped the picture postcard into my bag
as I left you and I didn't know why, what it meant

that it meant probably nothing.

KISSING TOADS

Eyes squint at the sun.
There is a dragon in my garden
drowning in autumn leaves.

My boy runs across fire to
fetch the gold in the greenhouse.
Lost socks grow to monsters in the

basement. There is a toad in
the bathroom. I speak
in guttural sounds learnt

from the internet and
wake in my overflowing
gutter – and fall sludge on

the milkman. There
is a toad in my bath.

A dragon sleeps in my garden

and I have learnt to dance
to the rats' songs
gnawing in my attic.

I switch off and on
pour hot and cold. There
is madness at my core

or wisdom? Hard to tell.

YOU MISSED THE BIRDS

I gave them to you. Nights full with the owl.
Mornings full of the crow. That woodpecker at Easter.
The robin perched on your fence.

You were angry that you missed the geese in the autumn
but you didn't, the sound of the skein had you cross
your room, you caught the last of them.

And you said, *I miss the quiet*
So I gave it to you
but you grew frightened of your own breath
drowned out your own voice with those made

of ones and zeroes.

All the things I offered you, you threw back.

Asked again and again for what you already had.

DEAR MUM

Looking out this window
I started thinking of Bill Withers
of how, when we were all confined
to our own five miles, we cared more
about our neighbours.

Learned the names of the birds.
Noticed our children. I started to cry
a wee tear that led quickly to sobbing.

It was quite something.

We put the tree up at the weekend
and even though it was only the fifth
we felt like we were the last to do it.
Och! It seems like everyone is depressed
and I suppose it did cheer me up
to come down to twinkly lights
Monday morning.

I just finished the Big Shop
I got you all the things you liked.
Then remembered you wouldne be coming . . .
I think I will put the red cabbage
in a Tupperware and leave it for you
on your front step, maybe I will sing
Lean on Me, through your letterbox.

We've done well to come this far
you said, it's true, and it'll no be long
they say, but I'll pop over, just to see you
Just to see you. I will put some tinsel
in my hair. Stay outside. Wave to you
through your window.

DAILY EXERCISE (AND SHOPPING ONLINE)

I have never gone from couch potato to 5k (except that one autumn) but I walk miles before breakfast. Yesterday he joined me, bouncing in, as I readied myself for escape, his small hand in mine. We were back in time for his online meet. The faces of his class appear in squares (revealing so much). But it was that beach walk I returned to at 3 p.m. when suddenly I started to cry whilst writing a work email, just the standard, *I hope this finds you* . . .

I told him as we were walking up the hill out of the estate, that you should spend a part of each day looking up at the sky. When he asked me why, I wasn't sure how to say for perspective, to tell my child that he is so fleeting.

His sister is doing a science lesson. Protecting the sofa feels too much of an effort, so she carries on reacting and refracting. I think about snoozing but instead spend hours on my phone, grazing like a cow until he calls me in for my tea.

In slippers I watch
the world slipping its moorings
browsing for flour.

PROPOSAL

I've all these years, building up like snow
growing drifts at our door, marking me
hermit – *fumbling prayer maker.*

I will become dangerous (to you)
a frozen lake, as its surface shatters

sharp ice, blood staining, sodden feathers

but I'm set to land, to make our home
in the thaw, *in the returning light.*

Fated too, to watch it float away
to be sinking at my desk in flood
water, marks on paper

Can you stand it?

SNOWDROPS

I've been following your boots down this path
each morning – this slow year of the familiar walk.

On Sunday, my Facebook memories
brought up a photo of you from six years back. You

in an orange coat I can no longer remember.
Triumphant by a clump of snowdrops.

This year's snowdrops crow in happy patches
we trudge past them with hardly a pause. I get out

my phone to take another photo of you. Later
while you play Minecraft with your sister

I scroll through photos to this photo on my phone. You
rushing out of the frame leaving me only snowdrops

(and the very edge of your boot).

LAPWINGS
For Melissa

I walked with my friend along an empty beach. Sitting two metres apart she told me her dreams. I told her mine. Together, we missed our mothers. Watched the lapwings in the salt marsh, the women swimming in the sea.

SPRING

I would be powered by only you

FIREFLY

You hibernated so long

dreaming of dancing
again with fireflies.

Dreaming above
Edinburgh streets

of warm water running over
your henna-brown feet.

Of geckos
climbing the white walls

of the mist like God's breath
rolling off the bay.

FLYING BATS

I was invited here
I am sure I was
to read my poetry
That's what the email said.

I've been writing a lot about trees
Oh! There is this nest I found in a hedge
blue wee eggs. A starling – *was it?*

*Aye, well. I was invited
that's what it said.*

Tonight, for all you lovely folk
I am unpacking my poetry suitcase – ta da!
The travelling poetry salesman. That'll be me
Roll up, roll up, going, going, going . . .

And they say after, they say, I love
how you spoke about found nests
as a metaphor for immigration
truth is, I've always been here

I was just writing about this wood
at the back of my house
about a nest I found.

How at night, I duck the bats
as if they might fly into my hair
even though I know, I duck.

Even though I know
they know this place

just as well as they know
I know this place. Still, I duck.

BEARS

In this street, there is an absence
of people. No one but the delivery driver
(in this wee town we know his name). *Leon* sidesteps
the daily walkers with his *Amazon Prime*. Bringing out
homeworkers from under their desks, greeting
their doorbells like family friends.

If this was night instead of day – bats, hedgehog, fox.

We light candles on grief days
and place them in our windows. We stood
and awkwardly clapped on those Thursdays past
but our wide road means we are not
the neighbours we hoped to be.

That Christmas invite from two years gone
still sits on the mantle. We are East Coast Scots
bears, masters of hibernation. We hold our children
in our caves now, but admit to each other in whispers
through the fence, *that nothing's really changed.*

We live in silence, noticeable, when the bird scare goes
or the call to work drifts over from the cement factory
but we had thought to first foot this year
do that *whiskyginsway* from home to home
that annual allowed noise.

Leon is bringing me a vinyl of Howlin' Wolf.
I thought on Monday, I needed the Blues.

He will keep the required distance.
I will hop back in greeting

the howl left between us.

OUTWITH (WRITING WORKSHOP ON ZOOM)

My headphones cancel the outside
and bring in the sound of the sea.

To think three of you are in snowdrifts
and I'm here in this damp dampening place.

I did not walk four miles to dig out my car
but my daughter came home with the dog
and I picked her coat from the floor
and hung it up on the peg.

As they talk I promise myself the woods.

He tells us his window is open in that English city
to let in the morning air.

I worry that doing that here would bring
in the harr.

She stutters through a poem, and he looks away
from his open window to his phone. I catch
the edge of it as she talks of starlings.

He acts the judge and executioner. *Big man.*
Showman. She offers a half-formed thought (it is beautiful).
He develops it to a bad exposure. Gives it up as his glorious insight.
She switches off her camera, thanking him for his cruelty. Taking
the awkward silence as confession he plays priest. He gives the good
    news
and I open another tab to read my emails. Out my window
my grandmother appears, walking with tigers.

He calls me out. I smile (hiding my teeth). Think to leave completely
but then she starts to talk about being a daughter and the farmer
    speaks of love
and if I try hard to focus beyond this dodgy connection I can almost
    make it out
of this glare to her hell steps, to a wetland in a city, his willow coffin
    and a rock face with names
etched in. But how do I tell them my grandmother has come
and I don't want to be here anymore? As I think to tell the farmer I
    have fallen in love with his lover
wrapped in a rainbow, he interrupts to tell us all, what he
has decided we are. Do you want the bad news?

I promise myself the woods.

The next day I am undone. I am nothing but noise.
But he brought my grandmother in from the harr.
And knowing he will see it as his victory. Knowing
she has been brought up here like bile. Knowing
all this, I let her dance for him. Her ink feet walk across the line.

REWRITES

I've been bunkered down
for so long, I forget myself.

I've been laying myself out
putting on slowly

the outside of who I am *for you*

(*this defining yellow, this funny beige*)

but we are not the same

(*nor fixed or so easily defined*).

A cacophony
of discordant voices

(warming up).

I am an orchestra held
which is readying to play

and I thought once, this
was the state of being

to be always
at the beginning

forever unfinished

POETRY PLATFORMS

Before I was told about you, I knew you
we would keep each other company
with *I spy* on long car journeys.

I found you jumping puddles, *as wide as oceans*
comparing Nana at the window to *a setting sun
dissolving sugar*, or *my last Rolo*.

Later, they tried to make you a stranger
when Sir ripped the flesh from your bones.
But you came in for me. Came back

as an alright? A hiya. A yell. A sigh
from the bottom of a well. Or was it a dark cave?
Or that forbidden corner of the back green?

We carry each other now
like soldiers carry each other
off the battlefield in films.

Like revolutionaries retreat
from the barricades in songs.

Like children come
when dinner is called.

I haul you on my back
and you carry me
in your arms.

You offer me ways.
Veils to dance wi

spittoons, bin bags
and platform shoes.

Poetry and I.
Poetry and me

it's all this I think
and other stuff too.

CHAPEL
John Muir Country Park

We have grazed on samphire
walked off your absence
replaced chapel for a sea breeze.

Told stories to keep them close
held a silence between us
– that felt like healing.

THE PERFECT SHADE

1.
It took me all this time
to find walls the perfect shade

for years I had thought it was green.
For a bit fashionable grey

fancied stark white in those beige
rental years but these four walls of deep

blue suit me, hold me –
somehow know me

and that's enough I think
for now, in my own home.

2.
It took him all those years
to finally paint his own walls

a disaster sure, clashing with everything
but walls that were his, put my picture
on a shelf – *a memory? an apology?*

Scrapbooked
my absence in a gaudy gift box.

Died in a room poorly yellow
but it was a surprise, his room

that he left for me to find.

GLORIOUS
For Adrian

1.
We spent a summer walking
Edinburgh. Telling tall tales.
Grew as tall as gods together.
Dominated the skyline.

We were glorious (everyone said so).

2.
I told you to take a moment
to love me this morning.
To put down your phone
and see me. I took your face
as known to me as my own.

We whispered, *I love you*
like prayer. Your smile
I took it. That moment

between us. Breathed it in
like the sea. Held it in
my lungs until I couldn't.

We forget.

MIND THE GAP

Mind that gap you tell
me over coffee. I can't
tell you that I've been
minding that gap
in you, since we first
met. That I've put it down
to your wondrous mind, the slip
stream, that writer's eccentricity.

Something is shifting in here
you say, pointing to your temple.

We go to the gallery, returning again
and again to this one painting

all wild sea, dark sparkle sky

but I remember now, that you
liked that cheerful painting the best

the one with the brightest colours.

MISSED TRAINS

1.
Nae seats, writing this poem
on my knees, wish I could

have chatted for longer but
I really needed to make it hame.

Now, I am crouched on my haunches
thinking of all the things I needed to say.

2.
You've been driving home your facts
missing the fact, I've missed two trains
and my tea, but the fact remains
I would've missed all the trains
to talk more poems wi you.

LEAVES FALL GOLD
For Beldina Odenyo

There is something divine in endings
when God comes to sit with you

leaves fall, gold on the ground.

The day the call came, *She is gone*
I lay on my bedroom floor

like a felled tree staring up
at the irreplaceable.

Should we cry it out to the sky?
Where should we take it – this pain?

I stared
at the empty sky

where did she go?

until it dropped low enough
to meet me, in the December sun.

And as this year closed
a bullfinch came

to sit, beautiful orange
in the bare winter branch.

I lit another candle
to light up flat memory

but the sun cut

in, leaving my ritual
redundant. There is nothing

more sacred, than the new day.
It's how I move forward

now that she has become
Everything.

The sky is so beautiful
today, I hear her laughter

in it. I hear it all the time.
I hear her in every line.

MURMURATION PASSES
For the ones we couldn't hold.

Smudge. Smidge. Smother
Sigh. Gurgle. Bubble
wand in a child's hand. There   there
then   not. A silence made
for ghosts to fill. Come back!
Let me see shadow strewn smoke trail.
Spell weaver. Witch maker.
Come back!
Let me see deep wave.
Let me see tide surge. Moon swell.
Breath held. Let me see child's play.
Come!
Let me see . . .
Child.
Fish Catch. Come
let me see child.
Drift. Fell. Sea gift. Come
Let me see!
Let me see!

BROKEN SHELL

He is tired now – I am just beginning to breathe.
White sand turns to pebble before the break

I send him off collecting – put out a blanket of our coats
his pockets are soon full and he returns – sitting close

sweet feather soft bubblegum breath suddenly, burst!

He shows me with ceremony – each pebble – sea glass – oyster shell.
I pull him in – look back at the sea – in his small hands he turns a
crab claw

over and over, over and over, over and over

leaving the pebbles, shells
and pink stone – in perfect circle.

I'm like a wave coming in – broken –

and he gives me back, like sea air.

DAY OF OUR DEAD

Masked and chittering under patio heaters
we eat the Sunday roast. This is our day
of the dead. Between a mother and daughter

a dead mother lies. I tell you in hushed holler
of a robin that I think has been with me
all year. I tell you that I saw it again

this morning. Still, on the handle
of our rusting wheelbarrow. Perfect
like a postcard. So much so I say

I think it was an imagining, *a haunting*
you say. This we find funny, today
of all days, to talk of ghosts.

CASSANDRA

We meet on a bench in the park. Drink rum in the cold. She tells us she is done wi coping. We get drunk on old stories. When the dark comes, we reach for each other's hands.

MUM'S THINGS

Blue Nun
Carrot moisturiser
Yves Saint Laurent
Pink lipstick
Blue eyeshadow
Gordon's Gin
Henna red.
Knitting basket
paperback pile
radio tuned to Radio 4.
Roxy Music
Joni Mitchell
David Bowie
kept in vinyl in the press.
Nurse's cape and
starched cap.
A flexible friend
O.U. course notes
costume jewellery
stripy tights
cake stands and
painted eggs.

THEM APPLES

I delight in you

as I would in a view
from a window facing South.

I turn to you for the light
rest in you like a house cat.

I would be powered by only you

if I could only store you right
– like apples.

PRESERVING THE SUN
For Kai

My furrowed brow boy
you love your stories
your Greek Gods.

Mythology tucked under your pillow.

You say
you dream in Ancient Greek
of sleeping in ruins.

You say
you only want a Ford Escort
a mattress and a map to Sparta.

And I think
I would preserve you
like a Lemon Sun
put you in as you are

hair like a porcupine
teeth too big for your mouth.
I would put you in vinegar and syrup.

Hold you to the light.

FIFTEEN YEAR HONEY

I tried to drink whisky for you
you got me a Glayva – *once you can manage that*
that adding in the honey. We're not really alike
you and I, but at night I can trace back
each wrinkle on your face. You are still
that boy to me. We do not really age
not to each other, not really. Though
I appreciate how the years have
folded in. We sit in the evenings
drinking our whisky, our bodies
finding their comfort, understanding
now, what that honey really means.

THE POET AND HER SON
For Joseph

I let him in for a cuddle
and he calculates the area of the room.

Tells me about prime numbers.

You're a prime number, I say.
Always so yourself.

Imagine a chicken.

I do. She is beautiful.

It lays five eggs.

Speckled. Brown. Olive. White. Blue?

The farmer wants to divide his eggs into even groups.

We're a unit of five!

What about Sam?
(Our dog)

Well then, we are six and you and I could be two.

Love you mummy

and he folds himself in.

Love you baby, I say

calculating the moment
multiplying it by division.

IT'S THIS
For my mother

the whole *Rive Gauche* of her coming
of how I would break to her
tripping over, shins scraped clean
blood dripping down in slow-going streams.

It's my screams turning her
to see me, sea glass.
To scooping me up, her darling.

It's this! It's this!

GREEN
After Mary Oliver

First to remap it / I fear I was drawn in border lines.
Gates with rotting signs. Trace indentation –

finger, feather, frost – father . . .

The lichen spume – the way green shatters and splints over time.

I hold a thrush with a broken wing.
Find a place in the airing cupboard
it dies without seeing the sky.

What have I done?

(the fragility of a leaf spine – insects under rotting timber –
remembering a truth – my mother)

forgive forgive forgive

My work is the work of loving/ the slow green on the Birch

(the way it begins – the way it ends).

ACKNOWLEDGEMENTS

I would like to thank the following publications for giving earlier drafts of my poems a home.

'Green' was published as 'My Work is Loving the World' in *Makar to Makar* (Tapsalteerie, 2020) edited by Jackie Kay.

'My Mum Wears Pink Lipstick' and 'Fake News' were published in *#UntitledThree* (Neu! Reekie! and Polygon, 2020) edited by Kevin Williamson and Michael Pedersen.

'The Way of Things' was published in *Gutter*.

'Six of One and Half a Dozen of the Other' and 'The Long Walk' were published in *The Stand*.

'Scotland You're No Mine', 'Pocket Money' and an earlier version of 'Leeds Cathedral' all appear in my pamphlet *Finding Seaglass* (Stewed Rhubarb, 2019).

'Abigail Says She's a Witch' featured as Poem of the Week in *Bella Caledonia*.

'Missed Trains' and 'Mind the Gap' were published as part of my poetry project *On My Way Hame*, published by Learned Pig.

I would also like to thank the Royal Society of Edinburgh and National Theatre of Scotland for commissioning my film poem 'Fragments' which has found form here as 'Lapwings', 'Cassandra' and 'Fragments, 2021'.

Huge heartfelt thanks to Edward Crossan at Polygon for challenging me to bring my poems together in this collection and for his editorial support and guidance.

And a massive hug and a pint or two are due to my lovely talented friends Jim Monaghan, Colin Bramwell, Iona Lee, Nasim Asl and Clementine Burnley who read early drafts and helped me hugely in selecting and editing this work. *Jim – I did it!*

This collection is dedicated to my wonderful friend Beldina Odenyo whose friendship offered me such belonging and was and will always be a constant source of inspiration. She read early drafts of this collection and we had plans to create a show inspired by the poems and we had started that process with a film poem made with the wonderful Beth Chalmers, with the support of Push the Boat Out Festival and National Theatre of Scotland. Now that you are gone, I offer up this collection to you Beldina. *I hear you in every line.*

I am blessed with wonderful friends and family and their love makes me brave. Thanks to all of you, especially my brilliant and gorgeous husband, my inspirational aunties and my wonderful mother and step-father.

Rob, you always held poetry and art at the heart of our family and I am forever grateful for that beauty and for the healing you gave me.

Mum, thank you for picking me up and dusting me off, for always being there and guiding me to safe waters. For reading to me, for reading with me, for always knowing my story could end well. My love for you is breathing.

To my writing gang in Dunbar, I love you all so much – without you? Och, it's not worth thinking about.

Adrian, fancy a walk?

And to my kids, *that's me finished now*!

A NOTE ON THE AUTHOR

Hannah Lavery is an award-winning poet and playwright. Her pamphlet, *Finding Seaglass* was published by Stewed Rhubarb in 2019 and her poem, 'Scotland, You're No Mine' was selected as one Scotland's Best Poems for 2019. *The Drift*, her highly acclaimed autobiographical lyric play, toured Scotland as part of the National Theatre of Scotland's Season 2019, and in 2020, she was selected by Owen Sheers as one of his Ten Writers Asking Questions That Will Shape Our Future for the International Literature Showcase, a project from the National Writing Centre and the British Council. In 2021, her second lyric play *Lament for Sheku Bayoh* premiered at Edinburgh International Festival to very positive reviews and she was appointed Edinburgh Makar in November 2021 for a three-year term. She is also an associate artist with the National Theatre of Scotland and one of the winners of the Peggy Ramsay/Film4 Award 2022.